THINGS I MEANT TO SAY TO YOU

WHEN WE WERE OLD

Things
I meant to say
to you
when we were old

Merrit Malloy

PHOTOGRAPHY
BY
STEPHEN R. SANDERS

DOLPHIN BOOKS
DOUBLEDAY & COMPANY, INC.
GARDEN CITY, NEW YORK

"Things I Meant to Say to You When We Were Old"
is the title of a poem in Merrit Malloy's first book,
MY SONG FOR HIM WHO NEVER SANG TO ME, published
by Ward Ritchie Press, Pasadena, California.

Many thanks to Jack Voorzanger for his helpful sug-
gestions and fine work with the photographs.

STEPHEN R. SANDERS

LIBRARY OF CONGRESS CATALOGING IN PUBLICATION DATA

Malloy, Merrit.
Things I meant to say to you when we were old.

I. Title.
PS3563.A4318T5   811'.5'4
ISBN 0-385-12326-4
Library of Congress Catalog Card Number 76–26353

For Young Paul

My sweetest love and affection
to the following friends . . .
Stephen Sanders
Chuck Morrell
Peggy Sandvig
Molly Malloy
Bridget O'Brian
Paul Monash
and to Patrick Filley, my editor,
whose encouragement was generous and real.

For Chuck on Easter, 1987,
with all my love,
S

Good title, but I haven't read the poems.

THINGS I MEANT TO SAY TO YOU
WHEN WE WERE OLD

. . . Not only because we may not
Grow old together . . .
But because we may not grow
Old at all . . .

MEMORY JARS

I know it's all too late in coming . . .
But . . . there were always things
I meant to say . . .
Things I always thought we'd share
Later . . .
When we were old . . .

We were so busy then . . .
Playing with children . . .
Who looked like me . . .
And slept like you
But who were never to be born . . .

We lived in houses then . . .
Designed on picnic napkins
And every conversation
Was as important
As a Cabinet crisis . . .

No . . . I couldn't tell you then
We were too fragile . . .
What we suffered from was love . . .
And more of it . . .
Would have killed us . . .

I remember when you'd stare at me
. . . The way mothers stare at sleeping babies
You saw me through a magic lens
That airbrushed all my imperfections . . .

God . . . I was beautiful then
Because you loved me . . .

We knew it was coming . . .

Every word had a direct effect
Like a bullet . . .

And each time
We shifted our weight on the couch
We squinched our eyes
As though walking
Through a mine field . . .

We pushed it away
As long as we could . . .
I'm sure people on Death Row
Do the same . . .

But . . . still it remained . . . and
We knew it was coming
And finally . . . just about midnight
We took eachother's hands
We held eachother just for a moment
And without another word . . .
You squeezed me . . .
. . . And I let it come . . .

"Good-by"

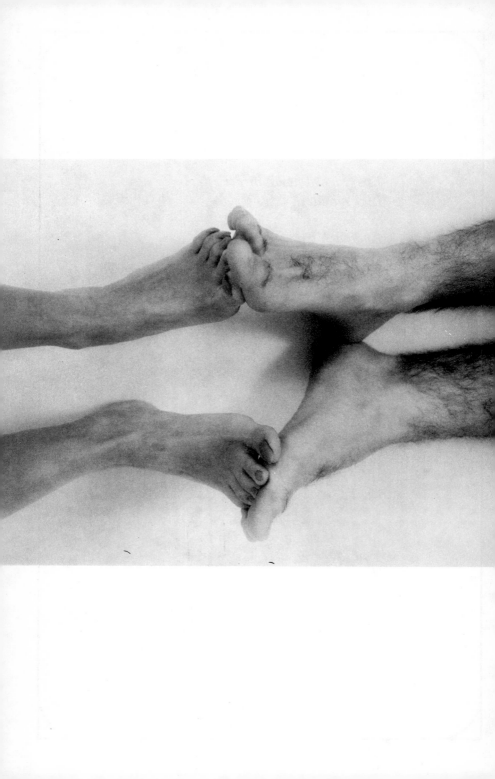

HEARING AID

He taught me how to listen . . .
Not so much to what people were saying to me
But to what I was hearing . . .

I still hear things
Filtered through my own private needs
I still sometimes hear
Only what I want to hear . . .

But now . . .
At least . . .
I know the difference.

THE FOX

We called them "Drugstore Cowboys"
They live on curb sides
And lean on parking meters . . .
Lit by the neon
Of the corner store . . .

They're not old enough to be bad
. . . And they're not young enough to be good
And they can't get away with either . . .
So they sit on skateboards
. . . And play with Duncan Yo Yo's
And live for the day they can buy a hot car
. . . Or join the navy or the world . . .

I had walked past that same corner for years
Unnoticed . . . anonymous
Even though I had known some of these kids
Most of my life . . .
I was twelve that year
It was long before anyone ever touched me
My breasts were just easing out of my chest
And the ache in my groin
. . . Was still in my imagination

"Hey fox!" they yelled.
"Wanna see my yo yo?"
And they laughed like children
Because they were . . .
"Hey fox . . . little fox . . . you're gonna be a hot
fox." . . .

I walked the few blocks to my house
A little differently that night . . .
I felt uncomfortable in my own skin
I felt transparent
. . . As though even strange cars and dogs
Could read my mind . . .

That night . . . alone
Locked securely in my room . . .
I stared at my body from every angle
Until it became familiar . . .
Slowly . . . I took off my clothes
And for the first time . . .
Without editing a nerve . . .
I seduced myself . . .
Instinctively . . . like a female animal

I experienced myself with wonder . . .
Let my fingers fall and fasten around my breasts
And even to the sprout of hair
That felt like down . . .
I trembled at the creature I'd become . . . "The
    Fox"
. . . And to think I'd been so dull
Just this afternoon . . . ˙

I can't remember who they were . . . those boys
I never walked past that corner again . . .
But for all the macho gained that night
And even at its price of pain . . .
I found myself . . .

And even today . . .
If I happen upon
A bunch of fourteen-year-old Drugstore Cowboys
Every time they whistle . . . I say thanks . . .

THERAPY . . .
THE REAR VIEW MIRROR

Memories grow out of memories
Like sprouts . . .
Each remembering
Is slightly distorted
From the one before
Like stories passed around a town
We become a victim
Of our own gossip . . .

That's what therapy is for . . .
To clear away debris
Around the center
To go back to the truth
However mean . . .
Or true it is . . .

And we believe our own fiction
. . . Perjuring our conscience
Until the truth comes back
To testify against us . . .

And yes . . . we were exciting
But not ever like the scores
I kept to keep us . . .
I remembered you with crayons
And I painted you for Paul
I remembered that I loved you
But I had forgotten . . .
That I didn't like you at all.

NEUROSIS OF THE LIVER

She thought men were saviors . . .
. . . And she looked for more in them
Than what they were . . .
Only to rescue herself
From those she wished
Would rescue her . . .

And isn't that the most tragic lie . . .
The lie . . .
Where we tell what we wished were true
And believe it . . . ?

She had an artificial memory
A prosthesis to a past that never was . . .
She was like a party
That no one ever went to . . .
Like a cure . . .
Without a disease . . .

And isn't that the greatest fear of all . . .
To be ready with the answers
. . . To questions that no one asks any more . . . ?

CONFUSION

Confusion
Is like a slow falling
A kaleidoscope of grays
That stays the same
The more it changes

A field of contradiction
Without gravity
Or form . . .
A rush of silent confetti
That belongs
To no one . . .

MERCY KILLING

I'm sure he doesn't know . . .
I mean . . . I've never told him
But somewhere there's a man
Whose face I've kept in frames . . .
Not the kind I'd keep in wallets
. . . Or on my desk
But mostly in my mind.
Where I store all the gifts I meant to give
. . . But somehow never have.

I've never touched him . . .
At least . . .
Not anyplace he'd remember . . .
Still . . . we make each other feel
Like awkward children . . .
In skin a size too small . . .

I fight his eyes . . .
The way frightened babies shield themselves
With shyness . . .
And helpless . . . like toy magnets
Our hands connect . . .
And suddenly I feel we are amplified . . . louder
. . . And in color
While all the others in the room
Remain in black and white . . .

I've never been so scared
As when he turned to kiss me
Sure everyone could hear it
Through the speakers
In their minds . . .

And yes . . . I want to go with him
But I know I never will . . .
It costs too much in broken bonds I've taken
. . . The price of pleasure doubles
For the price of pain you leave at home

And so we let those feelings die
. . . Like hopeless seeds
That were born without a chance

I can't think of anything
More worthy
of Euthanasia . . .

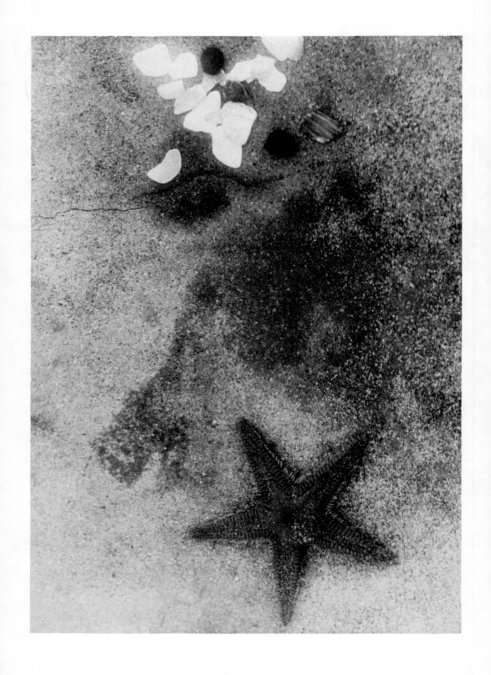

Whatever we say
We're always telling eachother exactly
What we want them to know . . .
We are always telling eachother
The truth
Even when
We're lying

AKA MARY MALLOY

Father Mark knew Mary . . .
I guess she was visible even then . . .
That part of me that took any chance
That anesthetized my logic
And kept me . . .
On the high wires
At the top of my life

It was that piece of me
That sat open
Like a nerve
Across the room from him
And he . . .
Consummate and subtle
Creating a wonderful tension
Simply by sliding into
Uncomfortable subjects . . .

And that part of me called Mary
Much too proud
To let her innocence be known
Tried to stop his hands
From discovering
That they were the first
To touch her

CONTINUED

How could I do that . . .
Let Mary out . . .
And put her in that room
With him
It was like sending a fly
To stop the Russian Air Force

But I must say . . .
She is clever
There isn't anything
She wouldn't do to get a laugh
. . . Or be remembered

Sometimes small innocent objects
Can fly into the most powerful of engines
And cause them to go down . . .
And crash

I guess that's what must have happened
He stayed around . . .
In his own way
For years after that night
Waiting for that part of me again
The elusive
Mary . . .

Every time I eat Rice Krispies . . .

I listen!

25

FOR MY CHILDREN

Perhaps . . . if memory were inherent
Like the color of your eyes . . .
Maybe you would know . . .
But all you knew for sure
Was what you felt . . .

Still . . . if it means anything
. . . And it will
Well . . .
Where I went last night
Wasn't nearly as important
As you were . . .
Although it must have seemed that way . . .

Yes . . . I do love him
And he does give me things
I couldn't get from you . . .
Feelings . . .
I can only share with a man
But you . . .
. . . You give me feelings
I could never get from anyone . . . but you

I hope it's not too late to tell you
That you're more important to me
Than any doorbell that ever rang . . .

I love you . . .

RESEARCH

For a time . . .
It was the only source of research I had
. . . My own experience
Even the most common of moments
Were tied with a ribbon . . . filed
And preserved like treasures
In memory jars

I know it's ridiculous
But I can remember the bumps
On my cotton polka dot dress
When I was five . . .

At fourteen . . .
I was an open wound
The slightest movement
Of a boy's eyes
Would create a breeze

So . . . at least for now
I can only hope that what happened to me
Can relate to what happened to you
That maybe our libraries are similar

Surely . . . you've been a child
Or know someone who's been one

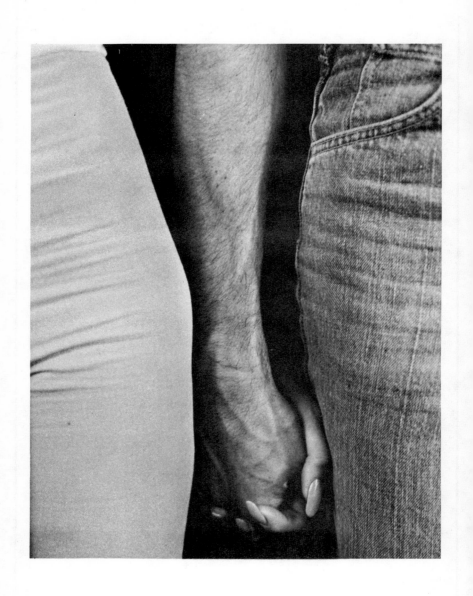

I found your jeans today . . .
. . . In the box with the Christmas lights
And old feelings
Came like parachutes
To rest me on the basement floor . . .

You know . . . I really liked you
I think you were the best playmate
I've ever had . . .
Even now . . .
I have some plans . . . left over
Like your jeans
That would only fit on you . . .

VARIATIONS ON A
DREAM

IMMORTALITY

In the beginning . . .
When I had too much of everything
. . . Even time . . .
I made a lot of promises
I couldn't keep . . .
Mostly to men whose business cards I collected
That I would throw like small change
On the dresser beside my bed . . .

The quality of life
Didn't matter much . . .
There was so much of it . . .

Later . . .
When I was too tired to start
And too young to stop . . .
I took out all the numbers
Preserved for evidence
In quantity . . .
. . . For the scrapbooks
In my ego . . .

Except for some of the numbers
That were still the same . . .
Everything had changed . . .
Except me . . .

I thought I had it all
That I was unforgettable . . .
And in a way I was . . .
They did remember me . . .
They remembered that I made promises
That I didn't keep.

.... Compromise ... is simply
When we change the question
To fit the answer . . .

It seems we're all being seduced
All the time . . .
By something or the other
And whether we acknowledge it
Or not
The least we can do
Is believe it

THE CHEST HUNTERS

They walk in groups
Of one . . .

They work their way like insects
Into your life . . .
. . . And body

And if you're the least bit friendly
They will hang over you and hover
Like homework
That you've put off . . .

With all the splendid men out there
Please don't fall for candy like a child
Left with bear tracks on your breasts
To validate their style

They walk in groups
Of one . . .

I knew when it happened . . .
I heard it . . .
Like a break in a circuit
I could still hear your voice
But it was smaller and not yours any more
And I could see you moving
Through the fuzz and static
On the screens that were my eyes . . .

There we were . . .
Almost there . . .
With just a foot to go . . .
And you the player-coach
Disregarded all our magic . . .
And called me in to punt
The only chance we had . . .

I knew when it happened . . .
I heard it . . .
And so did you . . .
You knew it . . .
We stayed with eachother
You and me . . .
But we were never together again . . .

CRIME AND PUNISHMENT

He didn't ask her where she'd been . . .
Or why . . .
He didn't want to know . . .
But he messed up all their bathroom towels
And scrunched all the covers on her side
As though someone had been there . . .
It wasn't fair

It hurt him so . . .
I know he wished she died
I'm telling you . . .
She tried

That night she loved his body
. . . And not him
Afraid that it might tell her where it's been
She didn't want to know
So she left some matches from a motel on his desk
To punish him
For what she imagined he had done
It wasn't fair

The truth is . . . she did leave
But not for real
And not for long
And stayed the night alone . . . At Motel Six
She didn't even use the phone

He waited for her that night
And when she didn't come
He poured two drinks and drank them both
And left them on the kitchen sink
For her to see and wash
It wasn't fair

It hurt her so
I know she wished he died
I'm telling you . . .
He tried

Fear can close you up so hard
That nothing can get in or out
The questions hurt too bad
The answers cost too much
So he married her for free
And he dropped all the charges
So did she

For all the questions never asked
They were the only answers left
And they didn't want to know
It wasn't fair

It hurt her so
I know he'd wished she'd lied
I'm telling you . . .
She tried

SUCCESS

I've laid my eggs . . .
The great pollen bearer
That I've been . . .

I thought planting seeds
Would grant asylum
From the past . . .

And in a way it has . . .
But now the harvest's grown so green
I'm afraid that it might last . . .

Looking back . . .
I don't know that I'd want so much of me
In exchange for less of you . . .

There are days when I would trade all I have
For just the simple joy . . .
Of wanting it again . . .

BUTTERFLY COLLECTION

It's that feeling
In the pit of the stomach
We call it butterflies . . .

It doesn't happen often
But Santa Claus
Can do it
When you're four

And certain men
Can catch you by surprise
Nearly scare you
Half to death
With no more
Than
Their eyes . . .

Labor pains
Can do it
Especially if they're yours
I've heard that people
Get them most
Just outside
Front doors

CONTINUED

They say that Dorothy had them
On her way to Oz
And phones . . .
Oh yes
They're a common cause

So add to your collection
It's harder now than then
The more you live
The less they come
And sometimes
Not again

I was the girl in the travel posters . . .
. . . You remembered
Waving from the billboards
With my apéritif . . .

And yes . . . I've been to Aspen
I broke my heart skiing
Trying to be an eagle
Forcing my body to obey
The images and dreams they weave
In travel posters . . .

I don't always know
What I'm going to say . . .
Until I've said it . . .

And it's not so much
What I say . . .
But more
How I feel
After I've said it
That matters . . .

Unfulfilled thoughts
Are like undelivered packages for me . . .

I almost never remember the exact words
Of a conversation . . .
But . . . I always know how I feel
After I've had one . . .

DÉTENTE

I know she married him
But it didn't take
The film was bad . . .
Or something

And tradition
Nailed her to him
And the babies
They did too . . .
And for years she tried to save them
But it was such a fight
He thought she didn't like him
And damn it . . . he was right

She prayed that they could be humane
Share the children's lives the same
But no . . . he said . . . not a chance
Let's tear them up
And use them
In advance
And now there are two little girls
Whose tortured father
Uses them as weapons
In a war that nobody wins

Small pink arrows they are
Sent to her tired and abused
With propaganda
They've done their best
Spitting out his anger
Bringing it to her in small
Mean sentences

It's time we face the facts—say it all out loud
There is no détente—It's just a word created for
     the press
It doesn't work . . .

I was lonesome for you tonight
. . . Lonesome for the old house
My own room . . .
My old covers . . .

How could you just go and die like that?
. . . And leave me here
                    . . . with all these strangers

I don't know what it's like
To be old . . .
But I think . . .
It's living long enough
To make a joke of the things
That were once
Breaking your heart . . .

On the highway
That leads from southern France
to southern Italy
Houses grow like moss
On the hillsides
Villages clumped like
Fungi above the road . . .

And there are no children
Just smaller people
Who were born
In handmade clothes . . .

History fits them all
Like a frame
As though they were preserved
By God
To remind us what we had . . .

I know it's distorted
My images are slightly American Express
We drove through their lives
As though their towns were paintings
In a great gallery . . .

Still . . . the canvas was so simple
And so powerful . . .
And the heavy fibrous ties that linked
Each face to each matched body . . .
I envied them their limits . . .
I wished and I still had mine . . .

Sometimes . . . like animals
We leave each other
For moments . . .
With quick contemptuous gestures
Of self-preservation . . .
And indifference
Turns into a brief enemy
People who . . .
Well-treated
Have been our closest friends . . .

I thought we were vaccinated
Against those small and terrible crimes
I thought we would inherit each other
And never let them beat us down . . .

But there is a place
Where you stop
And I begin . . .
Where I cannot edit my life
To fit you . . .
And you me . . .

6/14/76

I planted a tree today
In the park on Beverly Glen
And when it's big and strong
We will have known
And loved eachother
A long, long time . . .

Writing to someone you love . . .
Is the art of capturing a feeling
Without killing it . . .
Subtle crystal words
Can shatter a man
And unripe baby birds
Dropped from the nest too soon
Can die

According to the Latest Study

Grandmothers are the
Main source
Of all forgiveness

There are two people
In upstate New York
Who have committed life
And were never apprehended

And the people most likely
To get things done
Are those who
Haven't found out yet . . . that
It can't be done

If you stay the night
Or go in the morning
You are just as surely leaving
So please . . .
Just go

And no
You cannot hurt me more
Or even make me angry . . .
I won't make it easy
I won't rescue you this time

If you leave . . .
It will be with your own courage
Not mine

So please . . .
Just go
And don't look so surprised
After all . . .
I've earned it

I always knew you would

Arguments

Stain me

CARCINOMA IN SITU

I think tension eats oxygen
It was difficult to breathe
In that room . . .

Somehow . . . you knew
They didn't like eachother
Their humor was brutal
And unforgiving
And not funny . . .

I knew it was the last time
We would see them together
It seemed they were old and tired
All of their obsolete
And useless promises
Were lying on the floor
Like helpless insects on their backs
Sure to die in time

Driving home
I remember we were quiet
Then you kissed me at the light
You made me promise to tell you immediately
If I ever had a wound that wouldn't heal
Or a sudden change
In a wart or mole

As much as he was afraid of failure . . .
I was afraid of success . . .

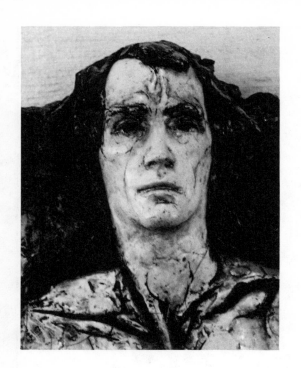

MISC.

I don't know how it happens
. . . But it does . . .

We put things aside
Even people . . .
To care for later
When there's time . . .

Meaning to get back . . .
But sometimes . . .
Even when we can . . .
We don't . . .

Unfinished paintings
Lie in basements
And we don't throw them out . . .
Not while there's still time
Left on the clock . . .

We were like the first eight bars
Of some great song
You and me . . .
Left in a piano bench

I always meant to tell you
And I always thought I'd have the chance . . .
But I never did . . .

I don't know how it happens
. . . But it does

For ten years I had a dog
His name was Trouble
But he wasn't . . .

He loved jelly beans
And wore a Levi shirt
And had his own apartment
No . . . it's true
He lived . . .
For a while
In a Volkswagen too

I don't know where he's gone
He never wanted to be owned by anybody
Determined to remain free
Looking back . . .
He was a lot like you

However we try to ignore it . . .
There are people who are special . . .
Lights do turn green
Just as they step to the curb . . .

He was one of them . . .
And I would press my nose
Against the window of his life
With the fear and interest
Of a ten-year-old reading Playboy *. . .*
It was the safest scared
I've ever been . . .

I do not mean to say
That there are those among us
Who are totally exempt . . .
But there are a few . . . with great courage
And style . . . who break loose
To amplify their lives
People with imaginations
That multiply like rabbits . . .
And however we try to ignore it
There are those among us who are special
. . . And he was one of them . . .

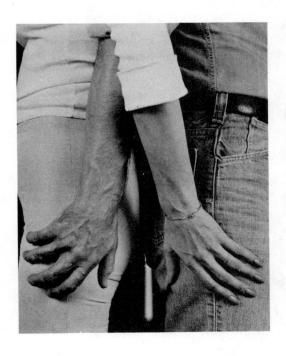

They write the master songs
·. . . In the only revolution
That makes sense . . .

They cut the social tissue
Through the membrane . . .
To the soul . . .

I always thought I'd join them
An illusion that sustains
I hoped that we were born alike . . .
But somehow
Not the same . . .

A STEP PROBLEM

I look at them . . .
. . . Our children
Separate and strong
And with more power against us
Than any God . . .

The conflict is . . .
That we compare them . . .
To each other
. . . And to ourselves

But they are separate
. . . They are not the same
They are not us . . .
And . . .
They are not ours . . .

We transfer to them
All that we wished for ourselves
So it is we . . .
That are bound to them
En route to ourselves . . .

Let's let them be . . .
Less like we are
And more like themselves . . .
Then . . . maybe
That will set us all free
From trying to be different
Than we are . . .

FRUITS AND VEGETABLES

Some men spoil like lettuce
. . . If not pursued immediately

Really . . .
Some lettuce . . . properly refrigerated
Can last longer . . .
And taste better
Than an average thirty-year-old actor

PORTRAITS

The art form is not love any more:

        It is just the promise of it . . .

Aren't we a pair?
You . . . the maker of movies
Me . . . the Irish poet
Imagine . . .
Laughing in every language
Like chameleons . . .
We were custom built for changing
But . . . staying the same

I wonder if we can get cavities
From too much pleasure
Constant orgasm would drive us mad
So we space it . . .
Like high masses .
And with each consecration
We become more devout hedonists . . .

Some people say it's a sin
To have too much and want more . . .
. . . But
They haven't been to the South of France
With you . . .

WITH BARBARA

With Barbara
It's not how or why . . .
. . . It's only when
And where

And we could say we'd gone to Oz
. . . Or simply just to Saks
and in that time
Could conquer Rome
Or maybe just the Bronx . . .
We've been high on Phanny's Phudge
And laughed so hard we died
And then got up and laughed some more
We hadn't even tried

If there was a limit
On good friends or time
I'm sure that we'd have passed it long ago
Cause with Barbara . . .
It's not how or why . . .
. . . It's only when
And where

BOZO

Once . . . in a rush
She wore two different
Color shoes
They matched perfectly . . .
It was her style

She had a car . . .
Or so it seemed
It had no birth certificate
Or insurance
We only drove at night

She saved me more than once
From permanent destruction
Made me study all one night
Just to get an A
That only changed my life

She was the only person
I ever knew
Who could dance to the news
And remember every word

So it didn't
Surprise me at all
To read
That her house burned down
The day she had her baby

After all . . .
She always could do two things
At once
. . . And always
Do them well

He lives here
In Paris . . .

If I wanted to . . .
I'm sure I could find him

But somehow . . .
It just seems enough
Knowing he is alive and well nearby
And that today
We were both walking around
In the same rain

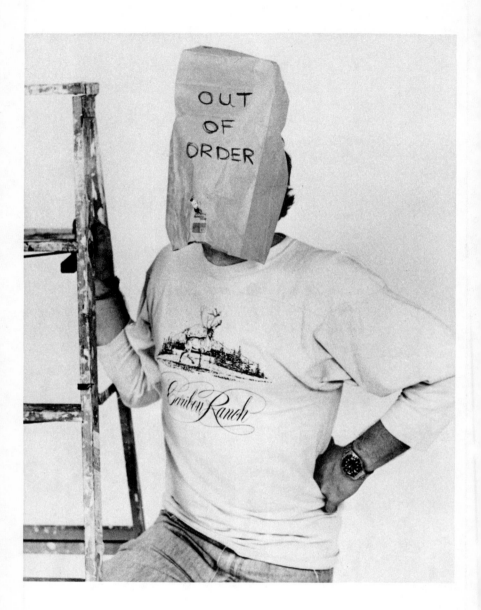

We've been children together
You and me . . .
We always stuck our fingers
In the pie . . .

And . . . you've been my family
I've been yours . . .
My last dime
Would be a phone call to you . . .

I had forgotten that you were a man
That I was a woman
My God . . . it was incest
When you touched me . . .

We're too close to risk
A physical pleasure . . .
You and me . . .
That's a gift
We only give . . .
To strangers . . .

SISTER ANNE

Every time I smell wintergreen
I see her there
Grading papers at the noon break
Young and small . . .
As though she were going to be a nun
When she grew up

I wondered if she had ears
. . . Or a past
I never saw either
Or asked

She didn't have to
But once she took me in the room
With all the other children gone
And told me that she loved me . . .
So did God
Even prayed for me sometimes . . . now
She didn't have to do that

And I grew up and left the church
Created my own God
And have since replaced him

And some people think of God
When they're in trouble or need help
Me . . .
I think of God
Whenever I smell wintergreen

I'm not sure that there is
Or isn't a God
I only know
When I was six years old
I met a friend of his . . .
Named Sister Anne
Who told me that he loved me

Now . . .
She didn't have to do that

I'm not sure
But I think
. . . The same people who believe
That marriage
Will legitimize
Lovemaking
Are . . .
The same people who believe
That divorce
Will legitimize
Anger

FRAMES

For a long time . . .
I only saw things in comparison

I only knew myself
In relation to other people
. . . And not in relation to who I am
Or was . . .
. . . Or why

I only saw you
In a line-up of men
For me to consider
. . . And choose

But once I loved my family
Without question . . .
Without a frame or social ruler
Without a measurement or accounting

We lose a lot in judgments
Mostly people . . .
But especially ourselves . . .

            Love is out of context
            It has to be . . .
            It's when we stop comparing
            That we love

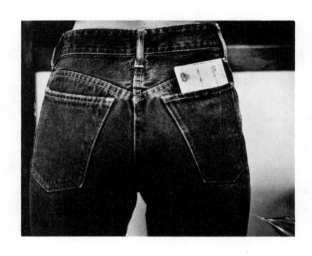

SPECIAL DELIVERY

Your letter arrived this morning
Unexpected . . . and years too late

I crowded it into my jeans
Sure to cover the broad, familiar strokes of your pen
Black as billboards
. . . And
As distracting . . .

Damn you . . . Just showing up like this
uninvited . . .
indestructible . . .
unavoidable
to leave your droppings
on a linen page
inside my pocket . . .

Each time the phone rang
It was an insult
Forcing me to fall back to the first word
And climb the pages again . . .

And in a way I'm proud . . .
That you could keep me all these years
It brings back some half-remembered pride I'd felt
In knowing that I knew it all along . . .
We grow to deserve
What we need to believe . . .
Since I've known you
I've been careful not to pray out loud
Wishes have a way of coming true
When you least expect . . . but

Damn you . . . Sneaking in like this
Unannounced
Insatiable
Inevitable
And me . . . with just
A sense of humor
To hold back the sound
of your footsteps
climbing the stair
just outside the safety
of my home . . .

OLD FRIENDS

They fall away . . .
They change their numbers
. . . And their names . . .
They evolve . . .
Some in pre-determined ways
Others become so unrecognizable
It takes proof . . .
To ever know you knew that at all . . .

We call them old friends . . .
Their faded names and addresses
Are in the little phonebooks we've since replaced
But somehow can't throw out . . .

They become caricatures . . .
Parts of stories we tell about ourselves
Some become a reference point
Of how far we've fallen or climbed
But mostly . . . they remain the same age
As we grow older . . .

The other day I read
That a playmate of mine became a doctor . . .
I'm sure it would be interesting to see her now . . .
But somehow . . .
I'd rather keep her safely where she's been
All these years . . .

. . . With me in a high school restroom
. . . Choking on our first cigarette . . .

FOR HER

When you'd call her . . .
To tell her you wouldn't be home . . .
I remember you thought I stayed quiet
Because she was a threat to me . . .

What you never knew . . .
And what I never told you . . .
Was that the threat came from fear of you: not her

After all . . . your lady and I
We had an alliance of sorts . . .

Often . . . I would think . . .
"If he can do that to her: what can he do to
        me . . . ?"

And now that it's over . . .
My feelings are with her . . .
And not with you . . .

It's just that . . .
Her loyalty to you . . .
Was more memorable
. . . Than you were

He was a master
A black belt in women
And he played each one
As she allowed

It didn't matter why
He needed to do it
Although . . . What you're thinking
Is probably right

It matters that he does it
And we let him
And he will continue
As long as we allow

So . . . the next time you find yourself
Trapped in a foreign bed
With a foreign master
Remember . . . it was you
Who wrote the script
He's just a hungry actor
Looking for the right part

It's not possible . . . I know
But I loved him that day at Jack's
I don't know why
And I don't know how . . .
It was as though . . .
We had grown up together . . .
Or spent Saturday mornings in bed . . .
I knew what it was like to have him
Lean over and whisper something
Purely and erotically our own
That only he and I would understand . . .
So . . .
That when he walked away
I felt vacant . . .
As though some adhesive in him
Had caught something in me
And ripped away . . .

I miss him . . .
And I don't even know him
I know it's not possible . . .
But it's true . . .

I would cry at his funeral

CHARLIE

I tried to find you in Nana's attic
. . . In drawings that she kept
And old sweatshirts
With your name
Inside the collar . . .

I've seen you in photographs
On dressers
And once . . . I read your letters
In mother's drawers . . .

But . . . you'll never be here
. . . In my home
You won't hear Mac laugh
Or Molly play the piano . . .
You'll never know Paul
And . . . You'll never know me

But I do remember you . . .
I remember you smelled like Life Savers
And Sen-Sens . . .
I remember you at your easel
With great lime crayons
And I remember the day
They pulled me away from you
In that white room
I remember your eyes . . .
*   . . . And I remember*
That I knew . . .

Sometimes his mind
Would leak out his mouth
And the words were so dead center true
I think it scared . . . even him . . .

He told me things I already knew . . .
But didn't really know
. . . Until he told me . . .

He wouldn't want me to mention his name . . .
That would be a violation
Of the gifts he gave me . . .
He lives in anonymity . . .
Maybe to be safe
But mostly he is like a cougar
Nourished by the land . . .
. . . And smaller animals like you and me

It's not that he doesn't care . . .
He cares too much . . .
And even that is not enough . . .
He trapped me with the truth . . .

It was a hard way to learn
Like tempting starving dogs
With poisoned steaks . . .
Expecting them to examine it
And ignore their instincts

I examine all my food now
Even the kind I eat . . .
The animals who live the longest
Are the ones who do not want too much
The ones who survive are aware
Aware . . . of the ones who don't
. . . And why

I have a feeling that one day
. . . He will find this book
And because it's mine
He'll turn the pages to see where I have gone . . .
And when he does . . .
I would want him to know how valuable he was
    to me
. . . And even though he wouldn't like it at all
And he wouldn't hear it
I would want to tell him that I loved him
And that he was a good friend . . .

FOR ROBERT

We were speared together
Joined
At the eyes. . .

We never planned on it . . .
Having fun
was inconvenient
And being happy
Was difficult to hide . . .

Love is noisy
It's easy to trace its original lines
Movements
Charge with neon
Love is proud of itself . . .
It leaks out of us
Even with the tightest
Security . . .

Under pressure
Our feelings crowded
Like political enemies
And soon . . .
We collapsed ourselves
Like carnival tents
And moved on . . .

But . . .
Thoroughbred sincerity
Does not come along
Every day
Nor does the quality
Of a man
Fit so splendidly
Into the afternoons
Of a woman . . .

I tell you
We were born
For that summer
Robert . . .
It was enough
To make a girl
Religious . . .

MAC

She told me once
She thought her mind
Was gaining weight
And that she couldn't talk
Because her tongue
Was broken
Once she couldn't
Go to bed
Cause she was stuck
To the floor
And there's more

She's easy
My child
Natural and free
Enough to know
That I'm her mom
And that I'm also me

She knows I'm a sucker
For a six-year-old clown
So she squirted
Through the room just now
And didn't make a sound

Behind my desk
I saw her paws
Sliding to a stop
"What are you up to"
"Oh nothin'" . . . she said
        "Just a lot"

What can she say?
She's not a scholar
No, the National Lampoon *is the closest*
That she's even been to Cambridge . . .

What did you expect? . . . That she'd be plain
All one color . . . and afraid?
Why does it surprise you that she's strong.
She doesn't have to die
Sweet Sylvia Plath already did that . . . it didn't
     work
She's more alive than ever . . .

She never meant to be your by-line
or your hero
It's just that her words
Were more visible than scars . . .

No, she's never had a lesson
Her only formal training was growing up in Jersey
It's as good a place as any . . . to be born old

So decorate her . . . if you must
Life is in public domain
But . . . as it is
She cannot bear her talent
It is more
Than she had wished for . . .

TOUCHÉ

I hadn't seen him
Since he left for Paris . . .
That was a year ago
He wrote and sent me hope
I didn't want . . . Then . . .
Called and took it from me
When I did . . .

So this morning . . .
When he called
I went to him . . .
And let him make the coffee
And the love . . .
For me it was charity
My offering for an afternoon.

He cooked me lunch
And struggled not to try too loud
. . . Or talk too small
He gave me back a ring
He bought once . . .
To buy some time from me
. . . When I had it

And then sweetly
Like a boy . . .
He begged me not to go
And gave me gifts of words
That smelled like promises before

I told him how I felt
That I would need some time
To maybe go to Paris for a year
. . . And then he smiled . . .

He already had his ending
And now . . .
I have mine . . .

Miracles
Are too loud
Overwritten
And
Too short

I don't believe
In Kansas
I lived too long
In
New York

Why is it that we always remember that people forget;
   But we always forget that they remember?

         I used to remember . . . but I forgot!

A NEGOTIATION

Some men keep an accounting
They want to know how many men have come before
(*Excuse the pun*)
And who bought the ring you wear on your third
    finger?
And who has been in this room before . . .
Seduced with caramels
and candles?

How many men have moved you
To write a page like this?
And how could you have loved them all
And still love me?

Well, it's not easy to explain . . . You see
Women are not exempt from human need, No
We are not a gift passed on from one body to the next
Autographed with fingerprints . . . Are you?

Yes, I have known and loved a lot of people
And some of them were men
And each one remains . . . And so will you
Now, What were you referring to?

Please don't ask me who has come before
Or if they'll come again . . . I can't answer that . . .
What we are to other people is irrelevant in this room
Where we know eachother in quarter notes
quick and resonant . . . temporarily exaggerated
. . . then gone . . .

I couldn't save boxtops for you
Or actively campaign
It's not my style
But . . . As a friend
I'm indestructible

We never could decide upon a name
Always . . . He was like a myth
Even as he was coming true . . .

I still feel him
Restless . . . round and round
like a dog circling
to find the right position.

Don't think I wasn't grateful
I was . . . even for the chance
to have a chance
Maybe it was the Tabasco . . . or

Who knows why a baby breathes
And then deflates into anonymity forever
As though the air was poison . . .

We'll never know him
And surely the other children will fill us full
With similar miracles . . .
But . . . whoever he was
He was restless
A renegade embryo
Unforgettable
Maybe only to the body that carried him
But . . . unforgettable
Nevertheless

A LETTER TO MY SISTER

If I thought I could
I'd tell you everything I've learned . . .
Even how to take life
In installment payments
Until you're old enough
To own your own

I've learned that
You can cure your age
With magic scissors
Some say that EST
Is the Lourdes of the spirit

One thing I know
Mr. Tooth Decay is dead
And there is no X ray
Strong enough to monitor the mortal sins
We didn't give to Father Mark

I can tell you this
Freedom starts in the lungs
Need forms a vacuum
Death cures pain
And the etc. is very important

When you're really down
Cold weather will be freezing
And somehow
When you eat alone
Food is more expensive

But don't sit in front of mirrors
Contemplating a cold sore
Sure that it's a sign from God

Just don't try
Just be . . .
Follow your center
Not my advice
Believe me . . .
Whiter teeth
And clear skin
Are not the answer

Religion is a malignant hope
I think . . .

Dogs no more
Than we imagine
Peace is available
And
Dreams are not fatal·

It's not easy to be eighteen I know
I've tried it
But somethings I know for sure
National Velvet *was only a movie*
And life . . . well
Life used to be a magazine

THE TRUTH

Discipline comes hard . . .
And mine is born in longer labors
The night before each manuscript is due . . .

At first . . . I fight
I don't want to exchange my pleasures
To pick up a pen
And stare at the white canvas
Of an unfinished book . . .

So . . . since you've come to me
In good faith . . .
I think you should know . . .
Some of this came hard and fast
Books like these are really no more
Than explanations of lives
Tombs in which we poets bury our dead
And most of mine are long at rest